Do Not Enter My Soul in Your Shoes

poe

Natasha Kanapé Fontaine

translated by

HOWARD SCOTT

MAWEN⟨I
HOUSE

We acknowledge the support of the Canada Council for the Arts
for our publishing program. We also acknowledge support from the
Government of Ontario through the Ontario Arts Council.

We acknowledge the financial support of the Government of
Canada through the Canada Book Fund for our publishing activities.

Previously published in a French edition as *N'entre pas dans mon âme avec tes chaussures*
by Mémoire d'encrier, Montreal, Quebec

Cover design by Jaaron Collins

Library and Archives Canada Cataloguing in Publication

Kanapé Fontaine, Natasha, 1991-
[N'entre pas dans mon âme avec tes chaussures. English]
        Do not enter my soul in your shoes : poems / Natasha Kanapé Fontaine
; translated by Howard Scott.

Translation of: N'entre pas dans mon âme avec tes chaussures.
ISBN 978-1-927494-51-6 (pbk.)

        I. Scott, Howard, 1952-, translator II. Title. III. Title: N'entre pas
dans mon âme avec tes chaussures. English.

PS8621.A49N4613 2015   C841'.6   C2015-902113-8

ISBN: 978-1-927494-51-6

Printed and bound in Canada by Coach House Printing

Mawenzi House Publishers Ltd.
39 Woburn Ave (B)
Toronto, Ontario M5M 1K5
Canada

www.mawenzihouse.com

Do not enter my soul in your shoes.
Gypsy proverb

In my country, I am in a far-away land.
François Villon

*I will save thee from afar, and thy seed
from the land of their captivity.*
Jeremiah 30:10

Prologue

FLEE NOTHING if you don't know exactly where to go.

A country, a man. You have loved. They crash together, like tectonic plates, to form just one single lament. A song of songs. A profound savagery to finally set fire to history, to your pain, to your legends. To the sorrows of all of you. Without these you wouldn't want to be you. Without these you wouldn't shout genocide.

Then you cross a river. Gaping.

Without turning around. Exile becomes a legacy. The St. Laurence fades red on equinox evenings. You flee Indian summers. Since, you are seeking to wipe away the water, unite your people, sing lullabies, or else, howl. You draw wild maps in the paintings of your soul. You write what you aren't able to describe. You . . . BECOME a mixed-race woman, sitting between two worlds, two shores, two histories. No, you dance.

Give voice to your people. Along with the others.

Unite.

Your song of peace.

Natasha Kanapé Fontaine

HOLD UP A veil of sun
to the gentle evening

soaking the possible
what can be

biographies woven
into memory

the downfall of time
katshinassimuna perhaps.

I HAVE LOST my way. The white compass is broken.
I walk along your detours, waiting to flee.
Inertias.
Welcome to my tired body, hungry for a parallel
world. I've forgotten the formula that broke through
the mist of the distant islands.
In return, rest in my devastated country.
I'd cook you partridge, if I could.
I whisper in summer bird.
Incantation.

*Smother me with moons in a vision from then
in a painting by Salvador.*

AN AUTUMN BED, I joined our two bodies
our peoples in discord

fettered
in the same pleasure.

PETAPAN KASHIKAT your sky dies out
I stretch out full length
on the land of your vespers
your azure finished with salt
gnawed

my offering.

THE HARES stand out
a fever
life birth
pleasure death
life

a fur withers
and takes flight.

YOU HAVE to be the possible
miam nanim
to make me out
catch sight of me

the Arctic steppes
will mix with our throats.

BLINDING humility
of a snow path
stabbed with doubts

I look for your brown silhouette
the smooth shadow
of your love.

THE TENT opened to a white dawn
immaculate work
original perhaps
the canoe camouflaged with sand appeared proud

purified it
it will take us tomorrow into *nitassinan*

come.

TAINTED sage

the rawhide
reveals
this blood
stretched by the woods of invisible
deer

my grandfather on the rapids

handed over through pride not famine
I contravene the law of hymns

wedding melded
snow and resin.

I TAKE root
on the underside
of my snowshoes
nishutina

atiman
the ether caresses
a last ice
for a last dance

brightened hours
absence abuses
tenderness.

AGAIN I see
your face and your eyes,
Indian reserves

the territory where I loved
being silent
burying my numbed fingers
run through
the trunk of your long hair
my untamed one
my ferocious animal

the territory where I loved
I go to ground
your river detours
mixed with mine
my work site
my dam of cement iron

ward off the sighs
barefoot.

I FOUGHT I thought
I touched your collar

diffuse torpor
distant season
where I joined you
the plain

my pace was going to
dash off to the open caribous

no runoff at all
on my lips.

I'M WAITING for the burning of the nerve
complete my awakening
my coat

the fires of dawn
will come
shatter the winds of your winter.

SUNS
rise
over the country of my birth

nipimutenan

there is summer as there are reservations
between us.

ROCK walk
clear resin
erected at dusk

atimi-tshishikau
detected between two white pages

abrupt track
snow falling in

TSHIUETIN
perpetrated

so
is my fate
already signed?

THE ANCIENT visions
mix with our laced fingers
evening kisses

alienated.

I SMOKE the walls where I crash
centuries of tobacco
falling in pipe dreams

my breath suffocates

flies off with
the sky of celestial
lanterns
clinging to stellar presences

the rhythm of voices and the drum
on the coastline of pains

I forgot the smell
of dried leather

setting for exodus
my heart.

THE FRAGRANCE of blazes
embraces my clothes

fiery
matshiteu

it leads to daybreak
the vanished breeze

drunken enormity
the smoked winter

I leave again.

My BONES on a translated fire

another language
the antlers of the running prey

the canoe goes astray
following ancient rites

without you I'll die of hunger!

contemplate
the evening skies
they are *assiu-mashinaikan*
windows on our demarcations

take silence forever
with me

the freedom falls quiet before

the huge.

THE WHITE birches
still grow

the rivers carry us
from one world to another

paths and dead leaves
coffee aurora borealis
boundary pages

white and red
beadwork

ishinakuan
pakushenitamun

the Indians act.

SHE HAD to walk, continue down the road,
climb back up the hill,
harsh old age!

tshuapateti a? I saw wolves for you
running along the bank on fearful nights
your anxieties devoured caribou of the end of the world
the marshes of your traditions
jostle then, illuminated by new dawns,
sleep
natuta!
upuamun minu-manitu! nanitam nikamu

tshipetuau a?
I drowned my pain
solitary giant of horror stories

mutilated *unaman*,
today.

Nipimuteti
anite minashkuat
ashit tshin

I remember
adverse winds
were rising

we had known
the standing dream.

THE TRAIL is marked with wet land

your footstep
is a man who is seeking
the shore
braided with white pearls

an eel
shines with miracles

the roots of the journey
have revealed the lines
of our full
hands.

My hips

your pelvis outshone
a shore; I lay down
so I wouldn't come back

I screamed my famine

torn from you.

I AM hanging
on your nerves

and my flesh
is emptied
of your name

your shoulder blades.

I AM peaceful

there is no wind
there is no more.

For the partridges fled
from the roads
I created traps

straps
for a single refrain

a single spring
for their little ones.

THERE, in the North! he'd cried out the sky
the leaves fly alone, before dying
a fire
burning from the inside
and I start laughing
make you smile
inside
on the inhabited tundra
it blows, a stifled shout
life
stretches in space
our lives cross
in catcher threads
I dream
the colours of the boreals
evening
filched from sacred mountains
melted into the immensity
of the subconscious

your fingers on my skin
my hair
beaded with mother-of-pearl

to get you to hear a folie bergère
tenderness is an adverse wind.

I HEARD your cry

you listened
the affliction of a tender bark

teueikan
nomad of my land
solitude heart

I heard your cry

retrace me
or I get lost

the sun dances
at night.

THE MOON forks
it has shifted the south, it wants to watch over the north
neither east nor west

you go against the current up the river
you hunt your heaven splits and
spills into my empty arms
the bark is crushed and burgles the messages
                                    hung in the wind

the birch trees have been made huge
shadows on the walls of my dwelling
when she is not there
winter follows on the heels of the court of miracles
I recount bibles while writing the ruined quills,
                                    the sand of the balcony

your dream ends where my body begins
I start on the light of your stiff foliage.

A FRAGILE necklace
an empty theatre

where the spectacle escapes beating its drum of eager glory

stops beating, to resume life

you stretch my straps over your fragile bed
to say that I will take nothing from my droughts,
but a true bitter mountain

in the sea my ink ices up and the rest of my eagles!

free vented invented fictitious *nipuamunit* are burst with
oceans

rowed miles to reach your island
Avalon tender tender tender
my mists fled onto your white arms

a vague word
and I drink in
and breathe out.

FIRST glow
I don't know
where I'm going
the sun sits right
over the sea

the irises
burned with light
I get drunk
on recklessness.

Too long
I carried my canoe
in urban forests
my country calls me
my country comes back to me
I complete my exile
for a trembling
return.

IN THE white morning
where January rises
the breaths of the Laurentian Arctic
surround the house as if in storm
the sisters breezes
illuminate the centuries remembrances

the blind open sea

Pessamit.

For Mushum

YOU SHELTER under your land
a pile of ripples
under your tent
and your cabin
raises a buried void
you then acquire the life that works
that is reborn from your ashes
ethereal memories
in convalescence.

YOUR WRINKLES of portages and straps
in confession
needle bones and tanning blades
recount each other legends
you kneel down
the dreams and the hopes in summer are in weaving
millennia-old motifs that display us
you are missing from the wisdom of wild realities.

GRATIFIED LEATHER
gaping entrails
old age oppressed in linear time
under the light
my course
against your landmark

find me!

where are you?
I am for you *petapan*
from the country where I lose myself
makanakau

you made yourself guardian
of our vestiges
nutshimit
lack in my eyes!

maiashtan
your empty canoe
evaporates

you wait for me
I won't come back.

THE INVISIBLE hunters
finally carried you off
with the north winds

here you are signatory of wild maps

Kesseu without sentinel
the day of the last fires

you dwelt in its trails and its fragile torrents
son of perpetual seasons
you leave with the canoe of your grandfathers

your brothers
waited for you on the other side
those impassable shores

and from the south, I remember you

Lhasa sings and opens the windows for me
my soul dances
with yours
where absence
widens

a sigh
barely audible
you watch over the parallel worlds.

———————

I KNOW,
it was you

tranquility
among the words scribbled
for you
nimushum

there are no terms
to beg for forgiveness

your tongue is human
it is without bitterness

my lament is a land
its people erased.

For Kukum

THE CIGARETTE lingers between your index and middle fingers
like so many others before
your lungs evaporate
when you embroidered your moccasins it was
                        memories on my skin,
where are my postcards? I scattered them

I would like sometimes for you to come back and reveal to me
those stories that are not told

stories forgotten, or simply put aside –
                        what is not said

the children are not yet born, but I'll tell them
                        you lived

                you'll know that people existed before them
                and that others will exist after

                        everything is a circle.

41

LEATHER ruts
hanging from the ceilings

come under the roof of the women
where they make
Indian moccasins

upessamu

the motionless brown
dolls
patient like seamstresses
with plain braids

the spirits of game
are scented with skins for sale

the entrance opens
on the sun of a summer month.

YOUR HOUSE gives me refuge
"a malnourished child"

I again see your passing
the trail in the woods
that led you to *Ashini*

he came back by bicycle.
he loved you for a long time
you know
until the very end
of his days

I still sew
your way
a nomad thread

a sedentary attachment.

THE FATIGUE of your knees
is wisdom for my people
your belly is empty when I'm full
when your face wrinkled with trails
now looks only at the light
under your eyelids
your knife now lingers only
on the softness of your palms

it no longer knows how to cut.

THE MOCCASIN felt carries
a hair of light
last wood shaving
kukum and her grand-daughter
colour prism fibrils

the leather of the craft shoe accumulates
in a black bag of family secrets

ruins

I look for a few words
from *innu-aimun*
under my tongue

I am of the city.

Is THERE anyone
to hear the cry of the drum?

I'm afraid
of the trembling of the world
I lie low
in the arms of *minashkuat*
as in the time
of my innocence

to play under the branches
silence
meshkanat

the giant birches
where my childhood
contemplated *Kukum*
and the springtimes

on *Kesseu* Street.

Medicine man
marked
with the sign of a hunter who himself

raised you to an uprooted nomadism

you learned the beaver you're the brother of the caribou
you learned the proud tanning
                                of the last territorial vestiges

you still look outside you see nothing now but
                                a repentant street
bent over its river decked out with palpable ripples
children awash in innocence
beaches devoured by barkless white wood
with spiritual seashells scattered in your suns
and your stars the camps of the household
are the survivors

our residential school stories.

THE CROSS of our
grandmothers' rosaries
strikes up one last dance

on August 15 each year.

Swirling, swirling
smoke evaporating
from my throat
with the falling drop
with the forsaken star
above Quebec City.

THE CIRCLES breathe the air oppresses us
the catchers trappers of nightmares
have made idle peaks

the animal spirits have set suns at our throats and

they have come back with our
dreams of perfection

the riverbank gave us back the canoes.

LAY MY HEAD on your knees
free the rivers
their embraces
to flee finally parallel and wreathed
emancipated tenderness
astray
adrift eternal just like always

famished for your day moons

disappeared the dreams of catchers
bring me back hold you back hold you
straight still far ahead
remembrance beaded with infallible beaches

you have for me the horror of wolves
the heat of fruitless summers
the cutting forests of the deaf
our goodbyes hopeless

helpless
lay my head on your knees.

IN THE NORTH of famines
the herds ice up
and expire
in the end
that lingers on

for me
nothing more in vain.

the light touch of sand bars
is a timeless
mist

my love.

EVERYTHING IS a circle
everything is a circle completing the pages
                              of history to repaint it
retranscribe the traditional legends

in the twilight tundra you breathe the bread of
your hunts incurred distant
your fire is a star among so many others
the mass is milky
a canvas frays then on the ceilings of your orbits
your searches cover tracks

stop breaking my erosions with your boats
                              let me finish!
my path still has steps to be taken
my stranger on my land!

do what you like as long as my brothers live
I'll read their shoulder blades draw them parallel
detect the voice of our fathers the roads blocked!
my alarmed ones without compass
my poorly armed.

YOU'RE A sky of unequal auroras
listless nostalgia, offending me
icy winter beaches desert of bitterness

the open country your calls my hours skinned with augurs
I bury, go! My fate is struck with it, tense, dried
to my resonant skins
ropes of our deafened baggage
the wooden circles are acidified by devoured herds.

COME MELT the blue of our broken jubilations
may they revive from a fire never seen, never heard
come sing the life-giving canopies
heal expire new existence dew
from your ashes fly away twice better
the enchanted cities will listen to the wing beats
of our wings in tune.

Your teeth laced up my vertebrae
your eyes are muddled with cedar
our bed of dead leaves is furrowed our hunts
purged of your cider
I would already like to run away
your walls surround me
it's pure air I should live on

my veins swollen with fragrances
your desire inviting my spirit to fade away
to close my eyes
and you press me to embrace you

I burned with your affections ardent my ashes.

MASHK^u
is sleeping still

you're a heaven hazy with opal images
you're my tender pale face
my catch and my grimy miracle
the trap where I fall in love

the ancestral air

you breathe me
give me back my book.

SEE WITHOUT looking,
look without seeing,
you have hands full of stories.

You rhyme with clocks missing from your azure
you write beaches and archipelagos
on my pale Indian woman skin,
oh lover of my sweet quivering waters
starved finished rivers, winter wrecks

your eyes are green spring leafy forests
older world
you lead to my black lands strong breaths,
breezes of salty summer, heat of glory
you love your fingers slip my emotion your lips
half open

boundless territory
settled let us live together our melancholy
broken in forgotten desired repressed

warmed with sick teas
my savage annihilated.

THE BEDROOM lulls me

white glimmer and pearls of mother
you your body
bark parallel to dawn

"the island of the dead"
where I run aground
where you take me

I fall in love

new journey
new world
toward another tender
wreck

the dusk of Sept-Îles
unearthed an exile
barricaded

behind my claims.

THE CLEAR embraces
watery at the window
for winter famines
April is tarnished just like that
I had you cold

your eyes ink glass rain,
the roads sly with days,
soporific slumbers to deceive the detours

the sprawling impotence the bitterness wearing
look after the white mornings when I make azure to you.

I WILL COME back then where I will be in exile there
even with the fir branches and the canine streets
even with the thousand-year laughs and the alcoholics always
even with the sky spiked with teeth of ebony wood
even with young women friends you recognize one just season
and they're gone the one after

and the realm of the dream made by the Spirits in the evening.

GLOSSARY OF INNU WORDS AND PHRASES

p. 1: *katshinassimuna* – lies

p. 4: *petapan kashikat* – the day is dawning

p. 6: *miam nanim* – as if against the wind, the other north

p. 8: *nitassinan* – our land

p. 10: *nishutina atiman* – they have two straps

p. 14: *nipimutenan* – we walk

p. 15: *atimi-tshishikau* – it is dusk

p. 16: *tshiuetin* - it is a north wind

p. 19: *matshiteu* – the bay, also a street in Pessamit called Metsheteu

p. 20: *assiu-mashinaikan* – map, literally book or letter of the land

p. 21: *ishinakuan pakushenitamun* – there is hope

p. 22: *unaman* – ochre, as in Rivière d'Ocre, also known as Rivière La Romaine on the Lower North Shore.

p. 23
nipimuteti
anite minashkuat
ashit tshin

I walked
in the woods
with you

p. 30: *teueikan* – drum

p. 32: *nipuamunit* – my dreams

p. 36: *mushum* – grandpa

p. 38: *petapan* – it is dawn
makanakau – a big island
nutshimit – on the land, inland
maiashtan – goes downstream with the wind

p. 39: *Kesseu* – street name in Pessamit

p. 40: *nimushum* – my grandfather

p. 41: *kukum* – grandma

p. 42: *upessamu* – silver lamprey (Ichthyomyson unicuspis),
origin of the name "Pessamit"

p. 43: *Ashini* – the main street in Pessamit.

p. 44: *kukum* – grandma
innu-aimun – the Innu language

p. 46: *minashkuat* – in the woods
meshkanat – on the road
Kukum – grandma

p. 57: *Mashk^u* – bear

Natasha Kanapé Fontaine, born in 1991, is a slam poet, visual artist, and environmental activist. (She has been dubbed the territorial slammer.) An Innu of the Pessamit community of the North Shore, like many Aboriginal youth of her generation she spent most of her life in urban areas. In 2013 the original French version of this book, *N'entre pas dans mon âme avec tes chaussures*, won the poetry prize of the Society of Francophone Writers of America. She figures on Radio-Canada's *Plus on est de fou* and has been on the lit!list of ten young writers to watch. Natasha Kanapé Fontaine is part of the new generation of a people rising from the ashes. She lives in Montreal.